THE BIG BOOK OF
BUTTS

EVA MANZANO   EMILIO URBERUAGA

nubeOCHO

Most of us don't really know

OUR BUTTS.

That's not surprising since they're mostly always covered. But even though butts might look similar, they're actually all quite different.

Every butt has its own personality. Some might be quite shy, while others are quite bold. But one thing's for certain: butts always exchange a friendly greeting whenever they see one another.

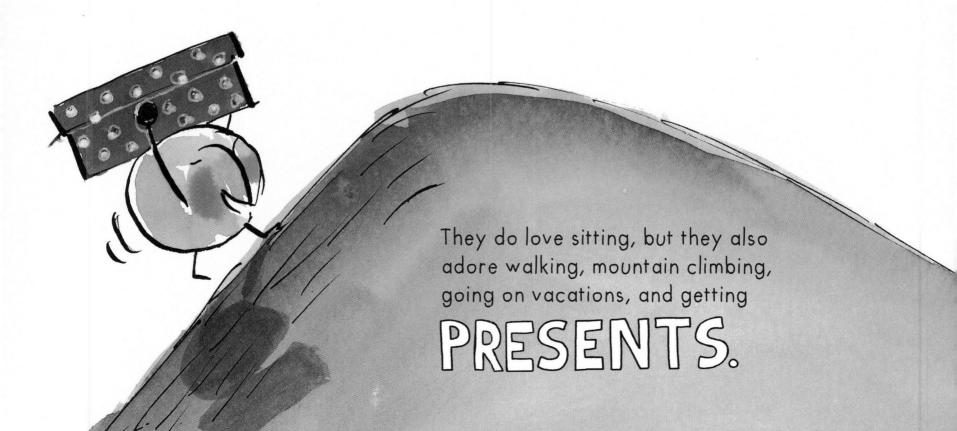

They do love sitting, but they also adore walking, mountain climbing, going on vacations, and getting

PRESENTS.

A BIT OF HISTORY

The butt as we know it today has its very own birthday. It first appeared in the

CAMBRIAN PERIOD

one fine day more or less...

540 MILLION YEARS AGO!

It all started when a few animals developed

A MOUTH

for eating and one to get rid of what they'd eaten.
This change allowed us to eat, grow, and increase in size.
Our brains were able to develop more.

Thus, having a "butt" made us

MORE INTELLIGENT.

WHAT IS A HUMAN BUTT LIKE?

We humans have a voluminous butt. At the base of the back are two squishy round cheeks, separated by a crack. Women's butts are often larger, because of a hormone called

ESTROGEN.

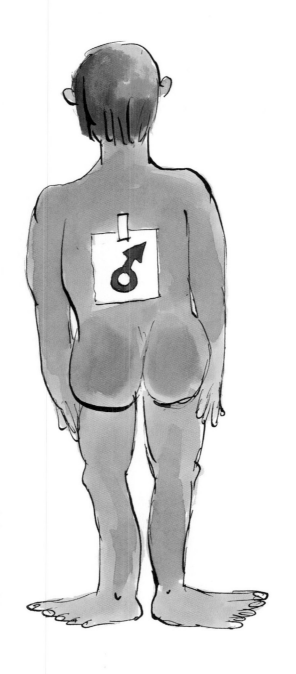

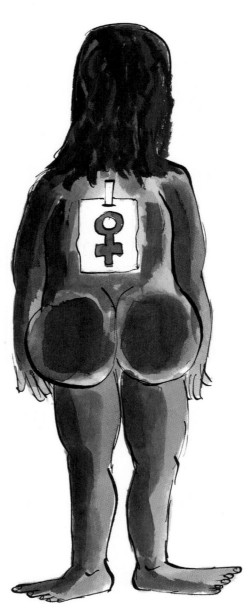

WHY DO HUMANS HAVE SUCH BIG BUTTS?

When we evolved from apes, the muscles in our butts helped us make the change from walking on all fours to

STANDING UPRIGHT.

That's how we were able to run long distances and survive.

THE HABITS AND CUSTOMS OF BUTTS

Humans can be pretty squeamish about butts, and they also have a lot of names for them: bottom, behind, rear end...

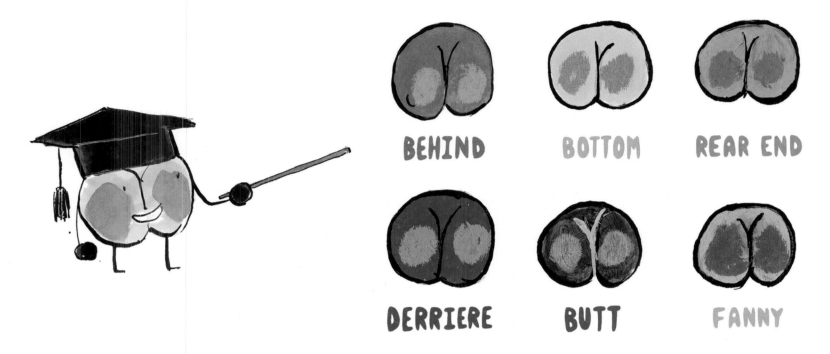

In some cultures, it's rude to mention them: bu— SHHH!
And it's not allowed to show them in public. But butts still show up everywhere.

Babies love running around completely

BARE-BOTTOMED.

Teenagers always check their butts in

THE MIRROR

before leaving the house.

THE BUTTS IN MY NEIGHBORHOOD

Francine the baker's butt looks like a big round

LOAF OF BREAD.

Herman, on the other hand,
sells fruits and vegetables,
and his butt actually looks like a

BELL PEPPER.

At school, Big Paul always says his butt itches,
and he scratches it with both hands. Then he chases us,
and we have to run away.

There is something undeniably
funny about butts, something
that just makes people laugh.

For that reason alone,

MONUMENTS

should be built in their honor,
in city centers and town
squares all over the world.

UNDERWEAR

Humans have a variety of different butt SIZES.
Some people wear BRIEFS and others wear BOXERS.

Underpants might have patterns of hearts, flowers, polka dots, stripes, or superheroes. They come in large, extra large, medium, small, and extra small. There are also plus sizes for

SUPER BUTTS.

BUTTS OF THE ANIMAL KINGDOM

Do plants or minerals have butts?
Can you imagine a mountain's butt? A volcano's?

A POTATO'S?

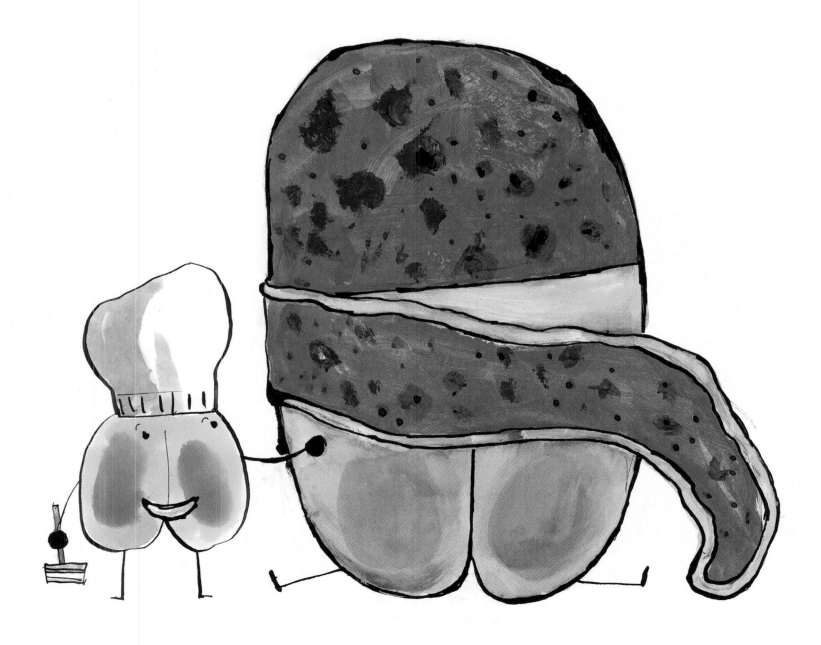

In contrast, insects, fish, amphibians, birds, and mammals all have butts (even if they don't all have **BUTT CHEEKS**).

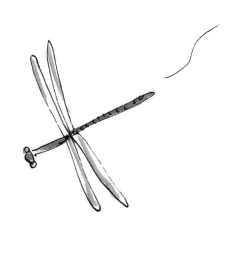

Butt cheeks, those squishy round things we mentioned earlier, are made up of muscles called the gluteal muscles

IN BOTH HUMANS AND APES.

BUTT COLORS

Butts come in almost every imaginable color. Let's take a look.

WHITE BUTTS

Polar bears have very large white butts, but because they're the same color as snow, they can be difficult to see!

BLUE BUTTS

The *Glaucus atlanticus* or "blue dragon" is a sea slug, and it has one of the smallest butts in the world. The blue dragon is poisonous, and it feeds on jellyfish. Even though people call it a "dragon," it's

BARELY MORE THAN AN INCH LONG.

PINK BUTTS

Pigs have famously pink butts, and they also have those cute little curly tails.

THEIR TAILS STRAIGHTEN WHEN THEY'RE IN DANGER!

RED BUTTS

Mandrills have red butts, and they're probably the most famous butts in the entire animal kingdom! Having such a bright butt makes them stand out in the green of the jungle. This helps the troop

STICK TOGETHER.

SPECKLED BUTTS

Giraffes have spots all over
their body, including on their butts!
They lay their long necks on them to

SLEEP.

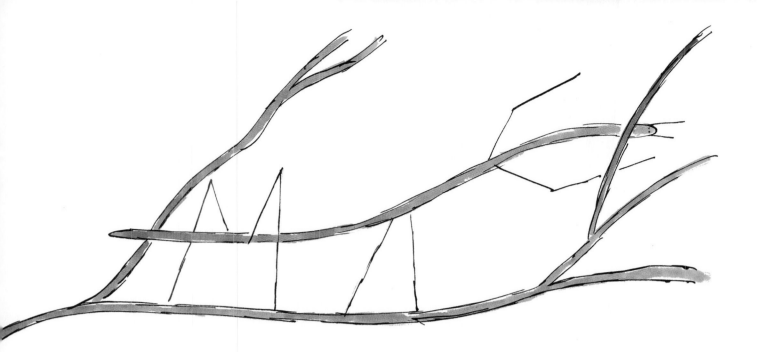

WOODEN BUTTS

Have you ever seen a stick insect? They're called that because...

THEY'RE EXPERTS IN CAMOUFLAGE!

You might even mistake one for a stick if you're not looking carefully.

MULTICOLORED BUTTS

Some animals' butts are a multitude of colors,
like the mandarinfish, the clown frog,
the halloween crab, or the regal ringneck snake.

The *Papilio xuthus* butterfly has an

ORANGE BUTT.

But get this: the most peculiar thing about its butt
is that it has two photoreceptors on it (a pair of "eyes"
that can take in and process light), which allow its butt to "see."

IS THERE SUCH A THING AS A TRANSPARENT BUTT?

The *Zospeum tholussum,* also known as the

DOMED LAND SNAIL,

has no eyes, and its entire body and shell are transparent.
It lives in caves and never comes into contact with sunlight.

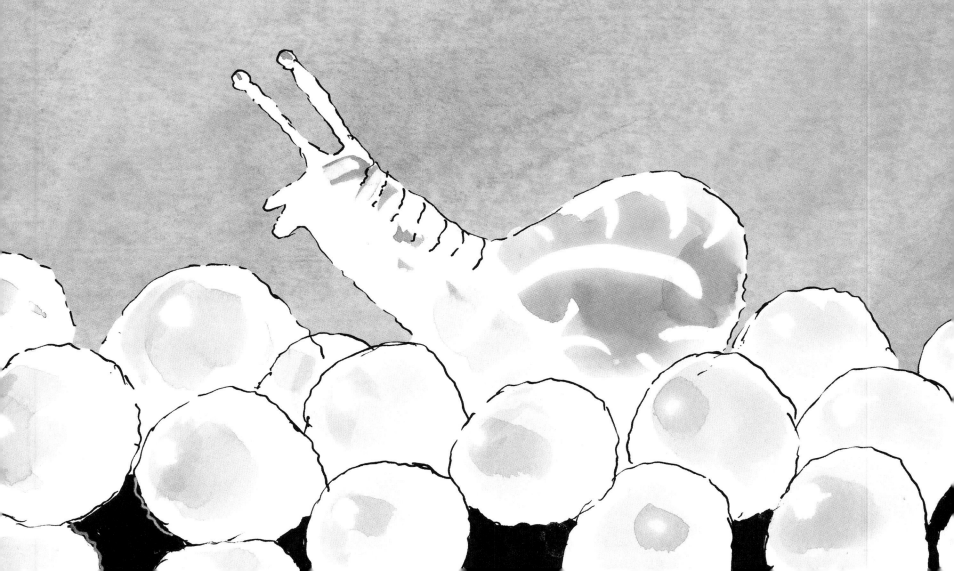

THE LANGUAGE OF BUTTS

The language of butts is fascinating. It might seem like they have nothing to say, but that's not true. Butts use nonverbal language to communicate through

CODED MESSAGES AND SIGNALS.

They have different systems for sending
and receiving messages through the five senses:

SMELL TOUCH TASTE
SIGHT HEARING

SIGHT

PEACOCKS love showing off their butts. The males fan out their tails in a bright display of color to attract females. Every feather has an "eyespot" or "ocellus" on it that shimmers in shades of green, blue and gold.

FIREFLIES have some of the prettiest butts in the entire animal kingdom. They actually light up! A whole bunch of twinkling butts lighting up the night sky sure is a sight to behold.

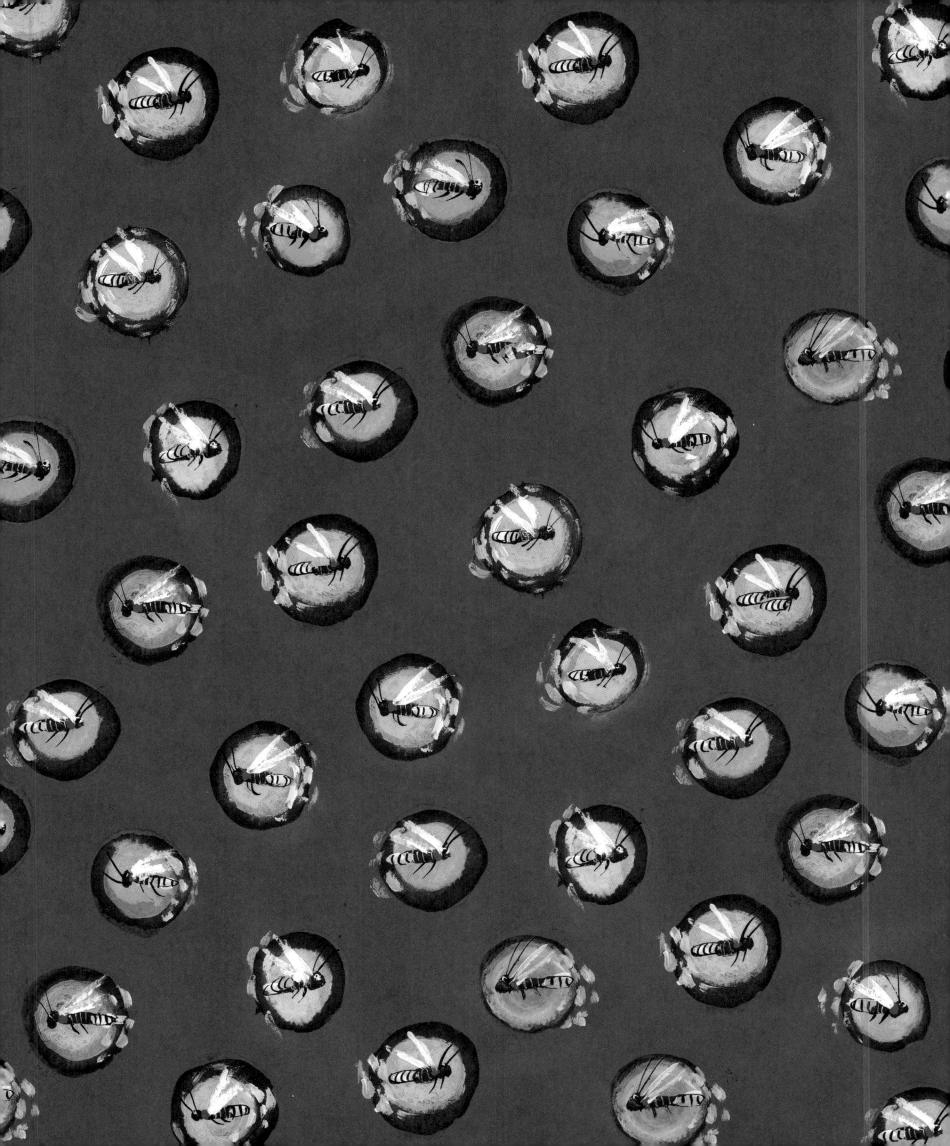

TOUCH

We experience touch not only through texture
but also through pressure and temperature. Butts can feel
rough, hairy, cold, hot, soft, hard, smooshy...

You can feel a ton of

WRINKLES

on an elephant's butt.

Or feel the

SLIPPERY BUTT

of a dolphin.

THE HAIRIEST BUTTS

belong to bisons and mountain yaks.

One of the coldest butts is that of the

ARCTIC HARE,

which changes color in summer to remain camouflaged.

SMELL

Hyenas live in very large territories, so their trick is to spread some of their excrement—which smells absolutely horrible—all around on the ground so that other hyenas can smell it and know where they are.

Dogs' sense of smell is between

times stronger than humans'. That's why they always greet one another by smelling each other's butts. They can find out a lot about one another that way!

HEARING

When a herring farts, the gas bubbles it releases let out an ultrasonic burst (a sound only the other herrings can hear). They use these farts to help orient themselves and to form their "shoals", or "schools of fish". Basically what that means is that herrings use farts to protect themselves!

AND WHAT ABOUT HOW BUTTS TASTE?

Actually, you know what? Let's skip taste. Ick!

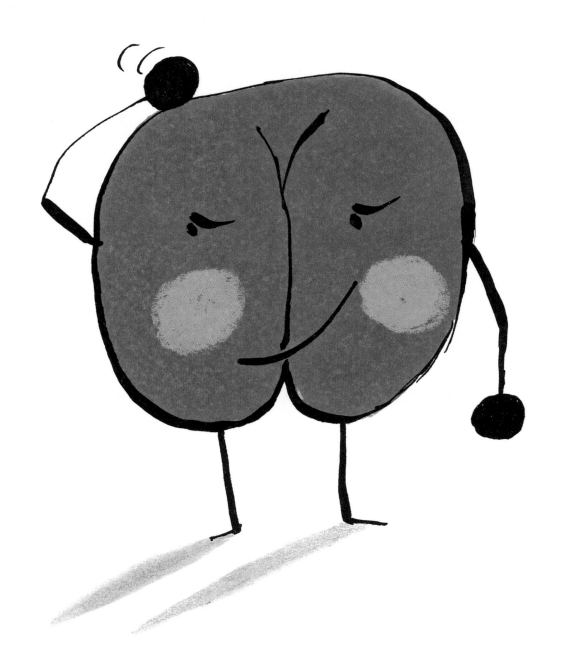

MORE MEMORABLE BUTTS

MOTORIZED BUTTS

The manatee, also known as the sea cow, is able to move through the ocean thanks to its farts. The bubbles it releases act as a motor.

LOCOMOTIVE BUTTS

Nope, no farts this time! Some animals, like the caterpillar, get around by moving their butts. They scooch it forward, smooshing themselves up, and then they stretch ahead.

(Try it out yourself, see how you do.)

DANGEROUS BUTTS

There are some animals that use their butts to attack! Bees and wasps have stingers on their butts. But remember, bees aren't dangerous if you don't bother them.

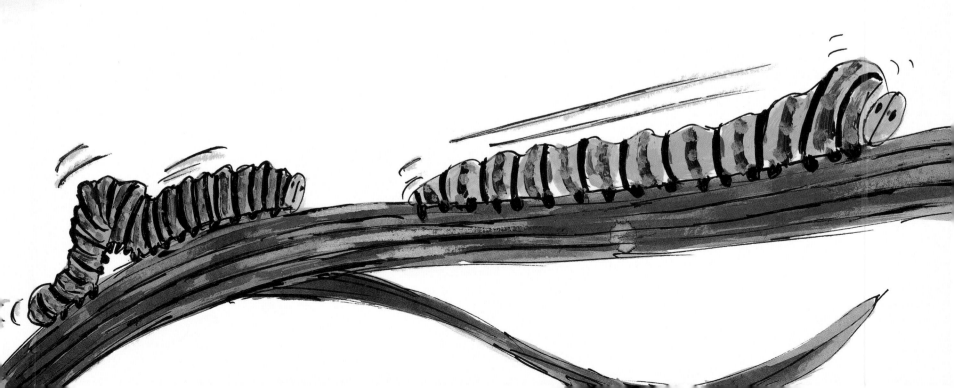

SPEAKING OF CATERPILLARS...

Caterpillars are the kings of butts. Some caterpillars have spots on their butts, and when they hold themselves upright, they look like snakes! They do this to protect themselves from predators.

Other caterpillars can use their butts as CATAPULTS.

They can launch their poop a distance of up to 40 times the length of their bodies!

NOSE BUTTS

The sea cucumber, a very strange-looking creature indeed, uses its butt to breathe. Some other animals even use this "nostril" as a sort of cave and live inside it.

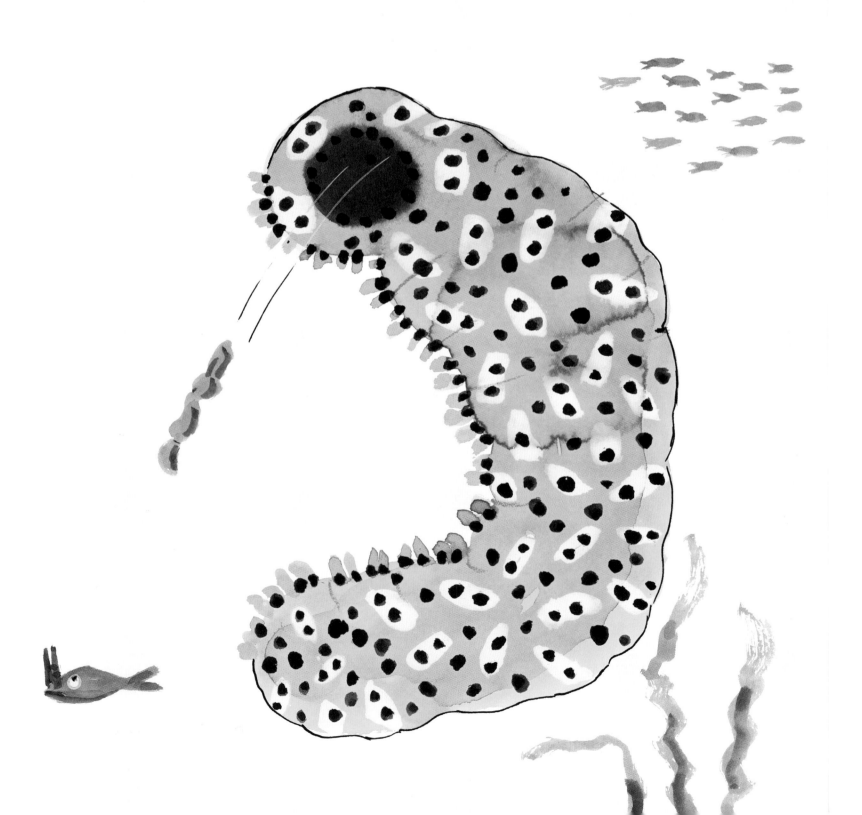

In conclusion, it's safe to say that

NO TWO BUTTS ARE ALIKE.

And never forget:

BUTTS LOVE TO DANCE, AND REALLY ENJOY IT WHEN YOU TAKE THEM TO THE BEACH.